BLUEGRASS
★ SONGS FOR UKULELE ★

ISBN 978-1-4584-1658-2

HAL•LEONARD®
CORPORATION
7777 W. BLUEMOUND RD. P.O. BOX 13819 MILWAUKEE, WI 53213

Visit Hal Leonard Online at
www.halleonard.com

Angel Band

Words and Music by Ralph Stanley

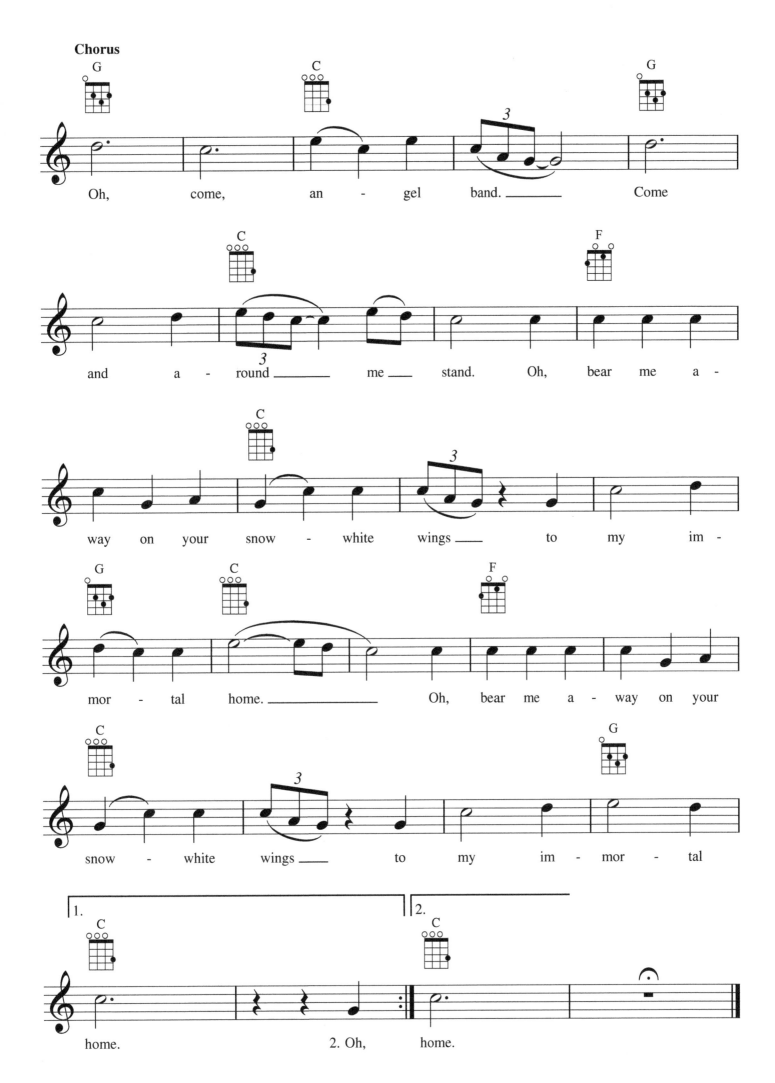

Blue Moon of Kentucky

Words and Music by Bill Monroe

First note

Chorus

Cash on the Barrelhead

Words and Music by Charles Louvin and Ira Louvin

First note

When the judge heard the ver - dict, _____
He let me call long dis - tance; _____
I saw a Grey - hound a - com - in'; _____

I was a guilt - y man. _____
she said, ___ "Num - ber, ___ please." _____
stuck up ___ my ___ thumb. _____

He said for - ty - five ___ dol - lars _____
No soon - er had I told her, _____
Just as I was be - ing seat - ed, _____

C   F

or thir - ty days in the can.   That - 'll be
she shout - ed out at ___ me: That - 'll be
the driv - er caught my ___ arm.   That - 'll be

Chorus

Bb   F

cash _____ on the bar - rel - head, son.
cash _____ on the bar - rel - head, son.
cash _____ on the bar - rel - head, son.

You can take   your   choice; _____
Not _____   part,   not   half, _____
This   old _____   grey   dog _____

___   you're   twen - ty   -   one.   No   mon - ey
___   but the en - tire   sum.   No   mon - ey
___   gets   paid   to   run.   When   the   en-gine

down, _____   no   cred - it   plan.
down, _____   no   cred - it   plan,
starts _____   and   the wheels won't   roll,

No   time   to   chase   you, _____   'cause I'm a   bus - y
'cause the lit - tle bird   tells   me _____   that you're a   trav - el - in'
give   me   cash on the   bar - rel - head; _____   I'll take you down _ the

1., 2.   **3.**

man.   2. Found a   tel - e - phone _   road.
man.   3. Thir - ty   days   in ___   the

Fox on the Run

Words and Music by Tony Hazzard

left   me   to   die   like   a   fox   on   the   run.

Like   a   fox, ____ like   a   fox, ____ like   a   fox, ____ like   a   fox _

To Coda

_____   on   the   run.

1. Now,
2. We'll

Verse

ev - 'ry - bod - y   knows ____ the   rea - son   for   the   fall, __
pour   a   glass __ of   wine ____ to   for - ti - fy   our   soul. __

____ when   wom - an   tempt - ed   man ____ down   in
____ We'll   talk   a - bout   the   world _____ and

2nd time, D.S. al Coda

Coda

Dooley

Words by Mitchell F. Jayne
Music by Rodney Dillard

First note

Verse
Moderately fast, in 2

1. Doo - ley was a good old man, he lived be - low the mill. ___
(2.) rev - e - nu - ers came for him, a - slip - pin' through the wood. _
(3.) I re - mem - ber ver - y well the day old Doo - ley died. __

___ Doo - ley had two daugh - ters and a
___ Doo - ley kept be - hind them all and ___
___ The wom - en - folk looked sor - ry and the

for - ty - gal - lon still. One gal watched the
nev - er lost his goods. Doo - ley was a
men stood 'round and cried. Now, Doo - ley's on the

boil - ers, the oth - er watched the spout.
trad - er when in - to town he come,
moun - tain, he lies there all a - lone. They

Foggy Mountain Top

Words and Music by A.P. Carter, Maybelle Carter and Sara Carter

Verse

ee.
1. Now, if you see that girl of _____
2. She caused me to weep and she caused me to
3. If I'd on - ly lis - tened to what my ma - ma

mine, there's some - thing I want you to tell her. _____
moan, she caused me to leave my _____ home; _____ the
said, I would not have been here to - day, _____

Tell her not to be wast - ing her time
lone - some pines and the good old _____ times,
ly - ing a - round this old jail _____ cell,

1., 2.

run - nin' 'round with some oth - er fel - ler.   If
I'm on _____ my way back _____ home. _____   If
weep - ing _____ my way poor life a -

3.

way.   If

D.S. al Coda

Coda

ee.

Footprints in the Snow

Words and Music by Rupert Jones

found her when the snow was on ___ the ground. ___
found her when the snow was on ___ the ground. ___
found her when the snow was on ___ the ground. ___

Chorus

I traced ___ her lit - tle foot - prints in ___ the snow.

I found ___ her lit - tle foot - prints in the snow,

Lord. ___ Bless that hap - py day that

Nel - lie lost her way, for I found her when the

1., 2.

3.

snow was on ___ the ground. ___

17

High on a Mountain Top

Words and Music by Ola Belle Reed

val - ley down___ be - low, ___   it was green just as
ev - er ___ think of me, ___   or has time blot - ted

far as I ___ could see.   As my
out your ___ mem - o - ry?   As I

mem - o - ry ___ re - turned, ___ oh, how my heart ___ did
lis - ten to ___ the breeze whis - per gen - tly to ___ the

yearn for ___ you and the days that used to be. ___
trees, I'll al - ways cher - ish ___ what you meant to me. ___

1.

D.C. al Coda

2.

⊕ **Coda**

Outro

I won - der if you ev - er think of me. ___

I Am a Man of Constant Sorrow

Words and Music by Carter Stanley

First note

Additional Lyrics

4. You can bury me in some deep valley,
For many years where I may lay.
And you may learn to love another
While I am sleeping in my grave.
(While he is sleeping in his grave.)

5. Maybe your friends think I'm just a stranger.
My face you never will see no more.
But there is one promise that is given,
I'll meet you on God's golden shore.
(He'll meet you on God's golden shore.)

I Truly Understand, You Love Another Man

Words and Music by George Roark

First note

Verse
Moderately, in 2

1. I   wish   to the   Lord   I'd   nev - er   been
(2.) who's   gon - na   shoe   your   pret - ty   lit - tle
(3.) Pa - pa's   gon - na   shoe   my   pret - ty   lit - tle
(4.) nev - er   lis - ten what an - oth - er   wom - an

born   or   died   when   I   was   young,   be -
foot,   and   who's   gon - na   glove   your   hand?   And
foot,   and   Ma - ma's   gon - na   glove   my   hand.   And
says,   let her   hair   be   black   or   brown.   But I'd

fore   I'd   see   your   two _ brown   eyes   or   heard   your   flat - ter - ing
who's   gon - na   be   your   own _ true   love   when   I'm   in the for - eign
you'll   still   be   my   own _ true   love   when   you're   in the for - eign
rath - er   be   on   the   top   of some   hill   and the rain   a - pour - in'

tongue,   my   love,   or   heard   your   flat - ter - ing   tongue.
land,   my   love,   when   I'm   in the for - eign   land?
land, _   love,   when   you're   in the for - eign   land.
down, _   down,   and the rain   a - pour - in'   down.

I

Chorus

tru - ly un - der - stand, you love an - oth - er man, and your heart shall no long - er be mine. I tru - ly un - der - stand, you love an - oth - er man, and your heart shall no long - er be mine.

1.–3.

4.

2. Oh, mine.
3. Oh,
4. I'll

I'll Fly Away

Words and Music by Albert E. Brumley

Keep on the Sunny Side

Words and Music by A.P. Carter

First note

1. There's a dark and a trou - bled side of life;
(2.) storm and its fu - ry broke to - day,
(3.) greet with a song of hope each day,

there's a bright and a sun - ny side, too.
crush - ing hopes that we cher - ish so dear.
though the mo - ment be cloud - y or fair.

Though you meet with the dark - ness and strife,
Clouds and storms will in time pass a - way;
Let us trust in our Sav - ior a way,

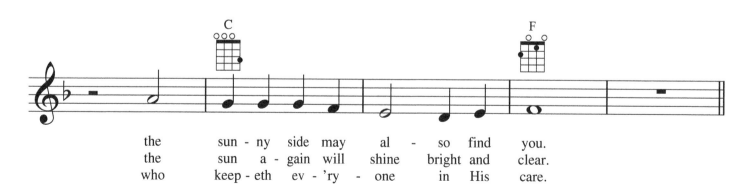

the sun - ny side may al - so find you.
the sun a - gain will shine bright and clear.
who keep - eth ev - 'ry - one in His care.

Kentucky Waltz

Words and Music by Bill Monroe

We were waltz - ing that night ____ in Ken - tuck - y, ____

be - neath the beau - ti - ful har - vest moon.

And I was the boy that was luck - y, ____

but it all end - ed too soon.

As I sit here _____ a - lone in the moon - light,

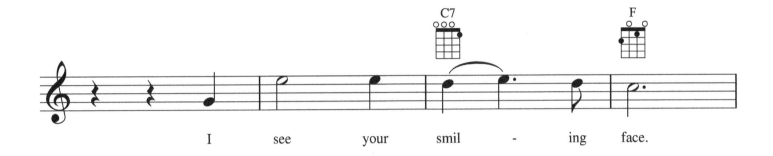

I see your smil - ing face.

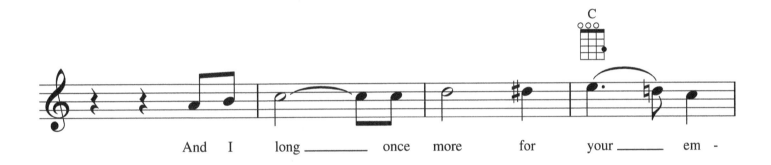

And I long _____ once more for your _____ em -

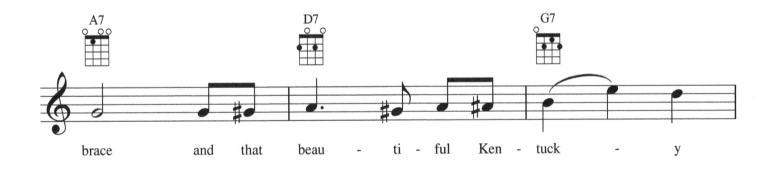

brace and that beau - ti - ful Ken - tuck - y

1. Waltz. We were 2. Waltz. _____

The Long Black Veil

Words and Music by Marijohn Wilkin and Danny Dill

First note

Verse
Moderately, in 2

1. Ten years a - go ___ on a cold, dark
(2.) judge said, ___ "Son, what is your al - i -
(3.) scaf - fold was high ___ and e - ter - ni - ty

night ___ some - one was killed 'neath the town hall
bi? If you were some - where ___ else, then you won't have to
near. ___ She stood in the crowd and ___ shed not a

light. There were few at the scene, ___ but they all a -
die." I ___ spoke not a word, al - though it meant my
tear. ___ But ___ some - times at night ___ when the cold wind

greed ___ that the slay - er who ran looked a lot like
life, for I had been in the arms of my best friend's
moans, ___ in a long black ___ veil she ___ cries o'er my

Midnight Moonlight

Words and Music by Peter Rowan

Chorus

moon - light, _____ in the mid - night, _____ in the moon - light, mid - night _____ moon -

light. In the moon - light, _____ in the

mid - night, _ in the moon - light, mid - night _ moon -

1.
light. _____

2.
light. _____

Once More

Words and Music by Robert Owens

Chorus

more, _____ to be __ with you, ____ dear, just for to -

night, __ to hold __ you tight. __ Once

more, _____ I'd give a for - tune if I ____ could

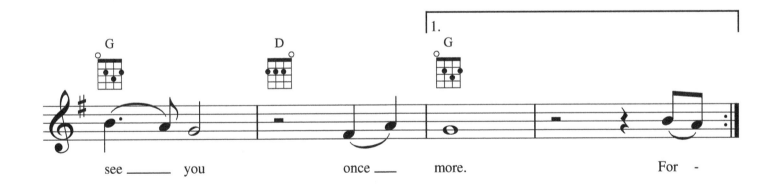

see _____ you once __ more. For -

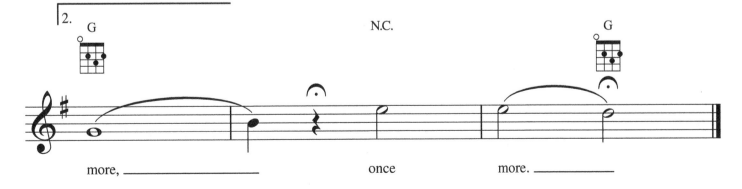

more, _____ once more. _____

Salty Dog Blues

Words and Music by Wiley A. Morris and Zeke Morris

Rocky Top

Words and Music by Boudleaux Bryant and Felice Bryant

Verse

2. Once I had a girl on Rock - y Top,
4. Corn won't grow at all on Rock - y Top,
5. I've had years of cramped - up cit - y life,

half bear, oth - er half cat.
dirt's too rock - y by far.
trapped like a duck in a pen.

Wild as a mink but sweet as so - da pop,
That's why ___ all the folks on Rock - y Top
All I know is it's a pit - y life

I still dream a - bout that.
get their corn ___ from a jar.
can't be sim - ple a - gain.

Chorus

Rock - y Top, you'll al - ways be home sweet home to

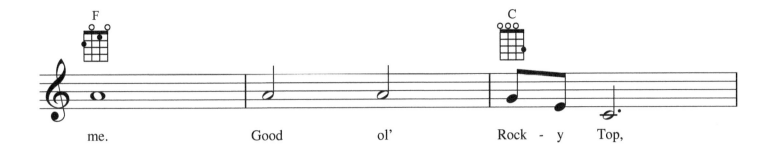

me.   Good   ol'   Rock - y   Top,

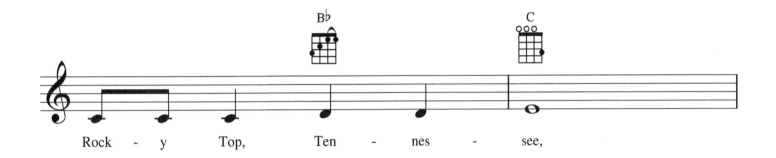

Rock - y   Top,   Ten - nes - see,

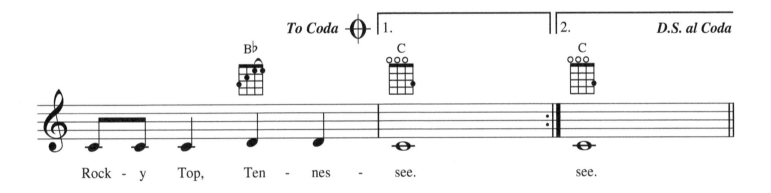

To Coda ⊕

1.

2.   *D.S. al Coda*

Rock - y   Top,   Ten - nes - see.   see.

⊕ **Coda**

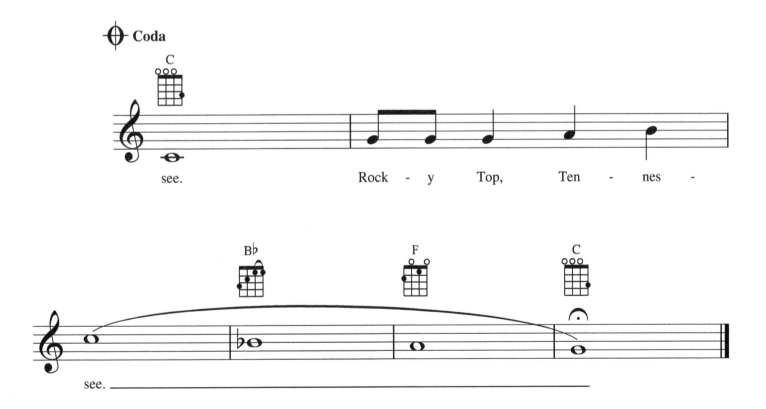

see.   Rock - y   Top,   Ten - nes -

see. _____

Sitting on Top of the World

Words and Music by Walter Jacobs and Lonnie Carter

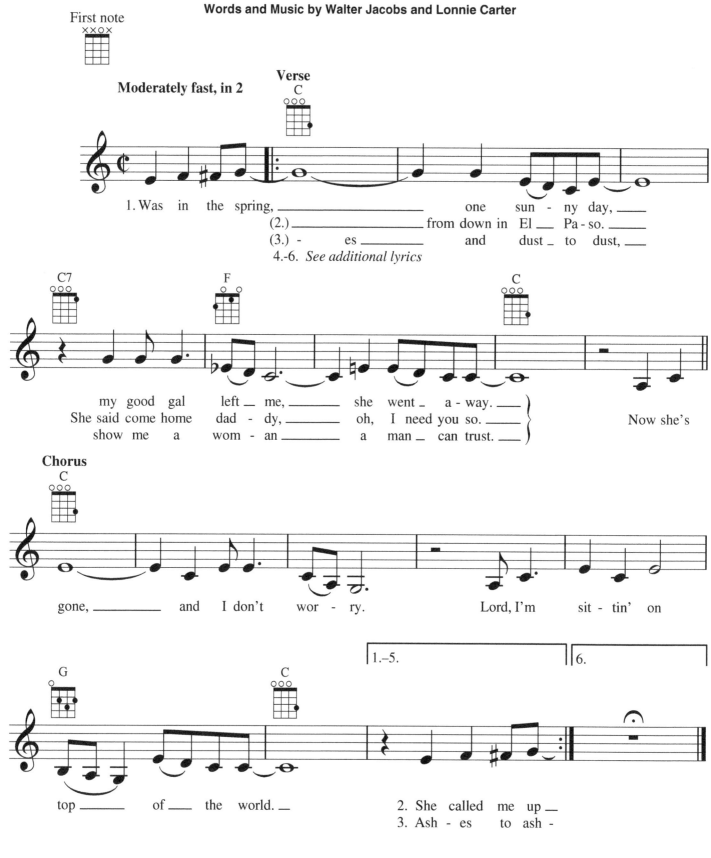

Additional Lyrics

4. Mississippi River
   Runs deep and wide.
   The gal I'm loving
   Is on the other side.

5. If you don't like my peaches,
   Don't you shake my tree.
   Stay out of my orchard
   And let the peaches be.

6. Don't come to me
   Holding out your hand.
   I'll just get me a woman
   Just like you got your man.

Turn Your Radio On

Words and Music by Albert E. Brumley

bra - tions com - - ing from the joy that His love can
liev - er lean - in' on the truths that were nev - er

bring, turn your ra - di - o on, _____
false. Get in touch ___ with God, _____

turn your ra - di - o on. Turn your ra - di - o

Chorus

on _____ and lis - ten to the mu - sic in the

air. Turn your ra - di - o on, _____ heav - en's glo - ry

44

What Would You Give in Exchange for Your Soul

Words and Music by J.H. Carr and J.J. Berry

First note

Moderate Waltz

Verse

1. Broth - er a - far _____ from the
(2.) call - ing you;
(3.) sil - ver and

Sav - ior to - day, _____
won't __ you give __ heed? _____
gold __ of this __ earth, _____

risk - ing your soul _____ for the
Must the dear Sav - ior still
more than all jew - els a

things that de - cay; _____
ten - der - ly plead? _____
spir - it is worth. _____

oh,   if   to - day _____   God   should
Risk   not   your   soul, _____   it   is
God   the   cre - a   _____   tor   has

call ___   you   a - way, _____
pre - cious   in - deed; _____
giv - en   you ___   birth; _____

what   would   you   give _____   in   ex -

change   for   your   soul? _____

Chorus

What   would   you   give, _____
                                   (in   ex - change)

what   would   you   give, _____
                                   (in   ex - change)

what would you give _____ in ex-

change for your soul? _____

Oh, if to - day _____ God should

call ___ you a - way, _____

what would you give _____ in ex - change for your

1., 2.

soul? _____

3.

2. Mer - cy is soul?
3. More than the

The Wreck of the Old '97

Words and Music by Henry Whitter, Charles Noell and Fred Lewey

Additional Lyrics

2. He turned and he said to his black, greasy fireman,
"Just shovel on a little more coal,
And when we cross the White Oak Mountain
You can watch old 'ninety-seven' roll."

3. It's a mighty rough road from Lynchburg to Danville,
On a line on a three-mile grade.
It was on this grade that he lost his average,
You can see what a jump he made.

4. He was going down the grade makin' ninety miles an hour,
When his whistle broke into a scream.
They found him in the wreck with his hand on the throttle,
He was scalded to death by the steam.

5. Now, ladies, you must take warning,
From this time now on learn,
Never speak harsh words to your true loving husband,
He may leave you and never return.

White Dove

Words and Music by Carter Stanley

First note

Slow Waltz **Verse**

1. In the deep roll-ing hills _____ of old Vir - gin - ia, _____
(2.) all so _____ hap - py there to - geth - er _____
(3.) years roll _____ by, _____ I of - ten won - der: _____

there's a place I love so _____ well,
in our peace - ful lit - tle moun - tain _____ home.
Will we all be to - geth - er some - day?

where I spent man - y days _____ of my
But the Sav - ior needs an - gels in
And each night as I wan - der through the

child - hood _____ in a cab - in where we
heav - en; _____ now they sing a - round that
grave - yard, _____ dark - ness finds me where I

With Body and Soul

Words and Music by Virginia Stauffer

Y'All Come

Words and Music by Arlie Duff

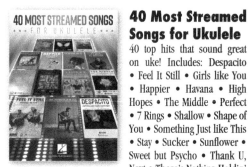

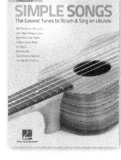